FIGHTING DISEASE

SCIENCE SPOTLIGHT

FIGHTING DISEASE

IAN GRAHAM

RSVP

**RAINTREE
STECK-VAUGHN**
PUBLISHERS

The Steck-Vaughn Company

Published by Raintree Steck-Vaughn Publishers, an imprint of Steck-Vaughn Company.

Editors: Su Swallow and Shirley Shalit
Designer: Neil Sayer
Production: Jenny Mulvanny
Electronic Production: Scott Melcer
Illustrations: Hardlines, Charlbury
      Graeme Chambers

Library of Congress Cataloging-in-Publication Data
Graham, Ian, 1953-
      Fighting disease / Ian Graham.
          p.   cm. — (Science spotlight)
      Includes bibliographical references and index.
      ISBN 0-8114-3844-9
      1. Medicine — Juvenile literature.   2. Immunity —
Juvenile literature.   3. Diseases — Juvenile literature.
I. Title.   II. Series.
R130.5.G73   1995
610—dc20   94-19981
                                                 CIP   AC

Printed in Hong Kong
Bound in the United States
1 2 3 4 5 6 7 8 9 0 (LB) 99 98 97 96 95 94

ACKNOWLEDGMENTS

For permission to reproduce copyright material the authors and publishers gratefully acknowledge the following:

Cover (top) Mehau Kulyk, Science Photo Library (bottom) BSIP, LECA, Science Photo Library
Page 4 (top) Mary Evans Picture Library (bottom) Kay Chernush, The Image Bank **page 5** (top left) The Hulton-Deutsch Collection (top right) Jane Burton, Bruce Coleman Limited (bottom) Michael Freeman, Bruce Coleman Limited **page 6** (top) Dr. Jeremy Burgess, Science Photo Library (bottom) Bernard Pierre Wolff, Science Photo Library **page 7** (left) S. Nagendra, Science Photo Library (right) Mary Evans Picture Library **page 8** (top) Larry Mulvehill, Science Photo Library (bottom) Martin Dohrn, Science Photo Library **page 9** (top) Jim Holmes, Panos Pictures (bottom left) Professor Luc Montagnier, Institut Pasteur, Science Photo Library (bottom right) Stan Osolinski, Oxford Scientific Films **page 10** (top) Adam Hart-Davis, Science Photo Library (bottom) G.I. Bernard, Oxford Scientific Films **page 11** (top) Mary Evans Picture Library (bottom) Michael Fogden, Bruce Coleman Limited **page 12** Larry Mulvehill, Science Photo Library **page 13** (left) Van Bucher, Science Photo Library (right) Geoff Tompkinson, Science Photo Library **page 14** (top) Bill Dobbins, Allsport USA (bottom) Walter Iooss JR, The Image Bank **page 15** (top) Petit Format, Nestle, Science Photo Library (bottom) Brian Hawkes, NHPA **page 16** (top) Bill Longcore, Science Photo Library (bottom) Tony Craddock, Science Photo Library **page 17** (top) Harald Lange, Bruce Coleman Limited (bottom) Grapes, Michaud, Science Photo Library **page 18** Professor P. Motta, Dept of Anatomy, University La Sapienze, Rome, Science Photo Library **page 19** (top) Simon Fraser, Science Photo Library (bottom) The Hulton-Deutsch Collection **page 20** Custom Medical Stock Photo, Science Photo Library **page 21** François Rickard, Allsport, Agence Vandystadt, Paris **page 22** (top) G.I. Bernard, Oxford Scientific Films (bottom) Dr. Jeremy Burgess, Science Photo Library **page 23** (top) The Hulton-Deutsch Collection (bottom) Howard Hall, Oxford Scientific Films **page 24** Stuart Bebb, Oxford Scientific Films **page 25** (left) Adam Hart-Davis, Science Photo Library (right) Hank Morgan, Science Photo Library **page 26** (top) Sipa Press, Rex Features (bottom) Hank Morgan, Science Photo Library **page 27** Dan Esgro, The Image Bank **page 28** (top) The Hulton-Deutsch Collection (bottom) Simon Fraser, Science Photo Library **page 29** (top left) Alvis Upitis, The Image Bank (top right) Kay Chernush, The Image Bank (bottom) The Hulton-Deutsch Collection **page 30** John Greim, Science Photo Library **page 31** (top left) Will and Deni McIntyre, Science Photo Library (top right) Ann Ronan Picture Library (bottom) Towse, Ecoscene **page 32** Ronald Toms, Oxford Scientific Films **page 33** ZEFA **page 34** (left) Cesar Lucas, The Image Bank (right) National Library of Medicine, Science Photo Library **page 35** (top left) Ann Ronan Picture Library (top right) Stephen Dalton, NHPA (bottom) Harry Taylor ABIPP, Oxford Scientific Films **page 36** Steve Proehl, The Image Bank **page 37** (left) John Heseltine, Science Photo Library (right) Allsport **page 38** (left) N.A. Callow, NHPA (right) François Dardelet, The Image Bank **page 39** Crispin Hughes, Hutchison Library **page 40** (top left) Mark Edwards, Still Pictures (bottom left) Tim Shepherd, Oxford Scientific Films (right) Mark Edwards, Still Pictures **page 42** (top) CNRI, Science Photo Library (bottom) Louise Lockley, CSIRO, Science Photo Library **page 43** (left) Kim Taylor, Bruce Coleman Limited (right) Omikron, Science Photo Library.

CONTENTS

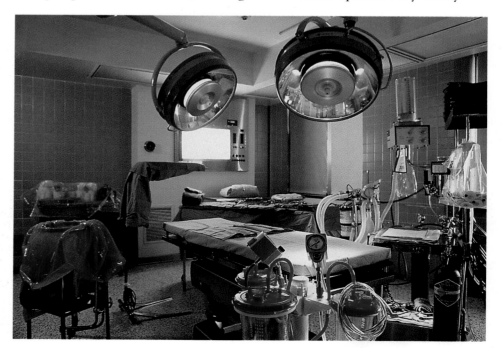

INTRODUCTION

We take it for granted that if we are unlucky enough to become ill, a visit to the doctor or a hospital will return us to good health. But this is quite a new state of affairs. Before the 19th century the causes of disease were not understood. There were no painkillers, no anesthetics, and few effective medicines.

An operating room in about 1920.

The microorganisms that cause diseases are very simple and they have existed in much the same form for millions of years. Fossilized bacteria similar to bacteria living today have been found in rocks 500 million years old. But the first people in the world were less affected by disease than people today.

Early man lived in small groups that had little contact with other groups. This meant that disease in one group could not spread easily to other groups. As modern civilizations began to develop, from about 6,000 years ago, people lived closer and closer together in larger and larger numbers. Then, in the 18th century, people in Europe started leaving their farming jobs and moved into towns and cities to work in the new factories that were springing up everywhere. They worked and lived very close together indeed. They did not understand the importance of cleanliness. Disease organisms could get into the food and water supplies and, once a few people were infected, the organisms could spread very easily

A modern operating room.

A 17th-century hospital (left) for patients suffering from the plague, or Black Death. The disease was spread by the bite of fleas carried by the black rat (above).

from person to person. Epidemics (widespread outbreaks of disease) were common. Some diseases spread all the way around the world before they died out. They were carried from one country to another by people such as merchants, soldiers, and sailors. Between the 11th and 13th centuries, a disease that became known as the Black Death, caused by the bite of infected rat fleas, spread from Mongolia through China to India and the Middle East. From there it spread by land and sea to Europe. The Black Death is thought to have killed 75 million people worldwide.

It was only in the 19th century that doctors began to learn what causes diseases. Until then, they thought diseases were either a punishment sent by God or the result of "miasma" (fumes) blown through the air from rubbish dumps and the rotting bodies of dead animals in the countryside. Since then, the pace of medical research has quickened and, in developed countries at least, many diseases can be treated or prevented.

Fighting Disease explores the human body, how it works, how illnesses and diseases affect the body, and what techniques and medicines are used to combat them. The book also examines some of the differences between disease in the developed world and disease in developing countries, and suggests how our individual life-styles can help to prevent or combat illness. **History Spotlight** boxes throughout the book highlight important people and events in history.

People in the developing world have always used plants to make medicines. In the future, the natural world may provide new cures to fight disease.

5

FIGHTING INVADERS

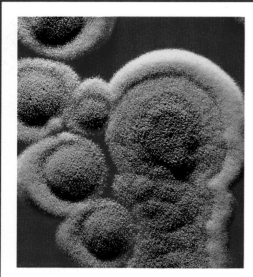

A close-up of the fungus that is used to make penicillin.

Until the 19th century doctors did not understand how infections were caused and how they spread. People died from injuries and illnesses that are easily treated and cured today. How did scientists find the answers to these medical mysteries and begin to win the battle against infectious diseases?

When diseases like cholera, typhoid, measles, or smallpox broke out in the past, they spread out of control through the population. Doctors were unable to treat them. In those days, surgeons wore their everyday clothes while they operated on patients and did not wash or change after each operation.

In France in the 1860s Louis Pasteur made a discovery that was to help doctors. He showed that fermentation (the process used to make beer) worked because of organisms in the air that settled in the beer and produced alcohol. When surgeons learned of this, they realized that disease-causing organisms might also be in the air. So they started spraying their operating rooms with an antiseptic spray. But they still wore their everyday clothes. A British surgeon, Thomas Spencer Wells, eventually realized what Pasteur's work really meant – that the germs that infected patients could come from anywhere, including the air, the surgeon's instruments, his hands, or clothes. Surgeons started to wear rubber gloves and face-masks, and sterilized their instruments in steam.

THE FIRST MANUFACTURED DRUGS

Cleanliness helped to stop infectious diseases from spreading, but once someone caught a disease, no amount of cleanliness would cure them. In the 20th century, doctors learned how to make drugs that would kill harmful germs and prevent many of these infections.

Doctors now know that the major diseases are caused by two types of organisms – bacteria and viruses. A bacterium is a single cell about 1/100th of a millimeter long by 1/1000th of a millimeter across – too small to be seen without a microscope. In the right conditions, bacteria can multiply rapidly by repeatedly dividing. They are found almost everywhere – in the soil and the air, on your skin, and inside your body. Most are harmless, but a few can cause diseases.

In 1928, the Scottish scientist Alexander Fleming made a discovery that was to change the course of modern medicine. Scientists often grow

Two children suffering from smallpox in Bangladesh in the 1970s. In 1980 the World Health Organization declared smallpox an extinct disease after a worldwide vaccination campaign.

6

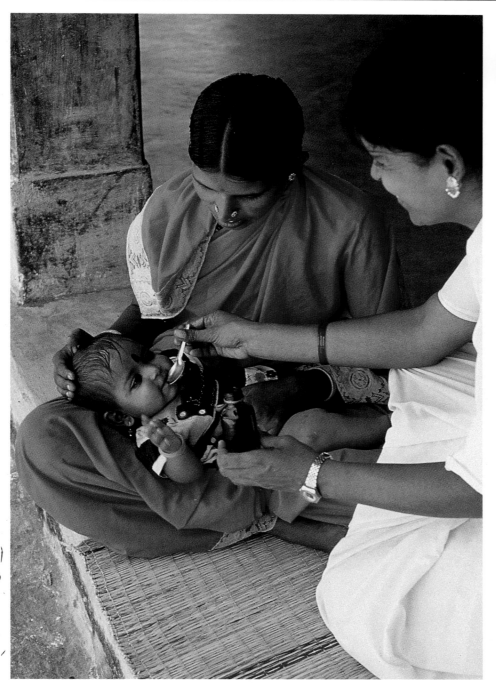

A nurse gives a polio vaccine to a baby in India. Polio is caused by a virus.

colonies (groups) of bacteria to study them. Fleming noticed that a blue mold called penicillium growing accidentally in one of his dishes was killing the bacteria next to it. By 1945 an antibiotic (bacteria-killing) medicine called penicillin had been developed from the mold. It works by bursting the bacterium's cell wall. A wide range of antibiotics has been developed since then.

VIRUSES

Viruses are even smaller than bacteria, as little as 1/100,000th of a millimeter across. Once inside a living cell, a virus can turn the cell into a factory that produces numerous copies of itself, which invade other cells and make even more copies. This damages and destroys the cells. Viruses are more difficult to fight than bacteria

because they hide inside the body's own cells. But in 1796, Edward Jenner showed that a person could be protected against smallpox with an injection of cowpox viruses (cowpox is similar to smallpox but affects cows). The body's defense mechanism is triggered by the cowpox viruses and is ready to fight the similar smallpox viruses. Jenner had invented vaccination.

THE ENEMY WITHIN

Some diseases attack the body from within. How do they strike at the heart of the body's defenses? And how are scientists trying to defeat them?

A human body contains billions of cells but develops from a single fertilized egg. It achieves this miraculous feat by cell division. One cell divides to become two. These two divide to become four, and so on. During the process, the cells become specialized. Some will form muscle, others form the heart, others skin, the brain, and so on. Throughout life, cells are continually wearing out, being injured, and dying. New cells are constantly needed to replace them.

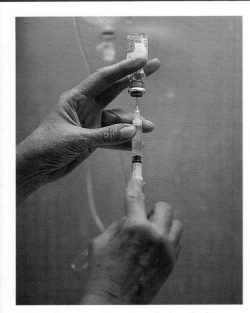

Chemotherapy – the use of chemical substances to treat disease – is used to help fight cancer.

Radiation treatment for cancer of the spine. The gamma rays can be focused onto a small part of the body.

CANCER CELLS

Normally, the genetic code inside the body's cells carefully controls the rate at which new cells are created and multiplied so that there are enough and not too many. Sometimes, perhaps because the genetic code in a new cell is faulty, the cell multiplies out of control. The growing ball of cells forms a lump called a tumor. Some tumors are small, slow-growing, and cause no problems. Other tumors grow rapidly and damage or destroy healthy cells around them. This type of runaway cell division is called cancer.

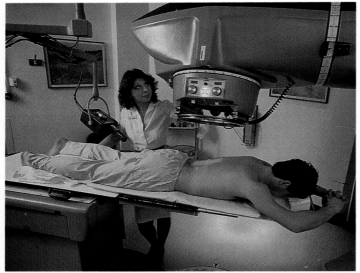

The immune system is unable to deal effectively with cancer because cancer is not caused by an invading organism, but by the body's own cells. However, there are powerful drugs that can kill cancer cells. Powerful doses of radiation focused on a tumor can also destroy the cancer cells. Many cancers can be treated successfully if they are identified early enough. Others are more difficult to treat.

A NEW THREAT

In 1981 scientists discovered a new disease which became known as acquired immune deficiency syndrome, or AIDS. In the short time since then, AIDS has spread all over the world. It is caused by a virus, the human immunodeficiency virus (HIV), that attacks the cells that defend the body – the body's own immune system. Once the virus has taken over these cells and turned them into factories to make more HIV viruses, the body is open to all sorts of infections. It no longer has the ability to defend itself.

Compared to other diseases that spread all over the world in the past, it is much more difficult to become infected with HIV. The virus is found in body fluids like blood, so fluids from two people have to be mixed together for the virus to spread from one person to another. It is most commonly spread by having sex with someone who has AIDS and, among drug addicts, by sharing hypodermic needles. Pregnant women can also pass the virus on to their unborn babies.

FINDING A CURE

One way of defeating AIDS might be to stop the viruses from entering cells in the first place. They can enter cells because their surface is covered with protein molecules that the body's cells can "recognize." The body's cells are covered with protein molecules, too. If the proteins on the virus fit any of the proteins on the cell's surface, then the cell accepts the virus as a friendly organism and allows it to pass into the cell.

A community center in Uganda for people suffering from AIDS.

Perhaps the body could be injected with large amounts of the protein on the cell surface onto which the HIV latches. The idea is that the viruses would link up with the proteins, but there would be no cells attached to them for the viruses to invade. The virus-protein package could then be dealt with by the immune system in the usual way.

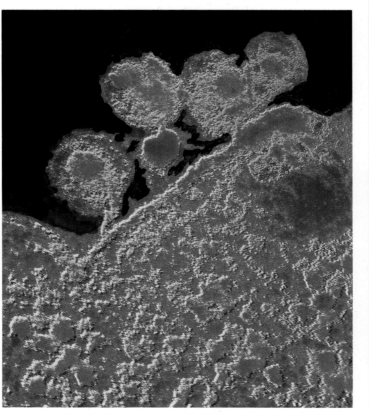

A view through an electron microscope of AIDS viruses (the round red shapes) on a white blood cell. The image has been colored by computer.

HISTORY SPOTLIGHT

Where did the HIV virus that causes AIDS come from, and when? Scientists have found an AIDS-like disease in monkeys. In the late 1950s, polio vaccines were made by growing weakened polio viruses in cells taken from monkeys. Some people believed that when these vaccines were injected into people in Africa, disease viruses in the monkey cells were injected into them too. Another explanation is that the virus evolved in monkeys in Africa, perhaps thousands of years ago, and spread to humans when they killed the monkeys for food. The virus would have spread as people began moving into the cities. After that, travelers could have carried the virus rapidly to other parts of the world. But we may never know precisely where HIV came from.

Did AIDS spread from monkeys to humans?

CHEMICAL DEFENDERS

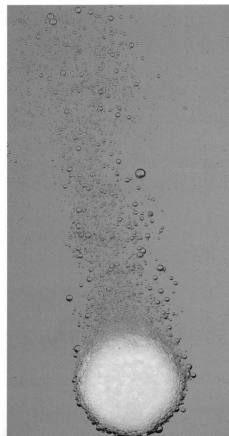

A tablet dissolving in water.

The ancient Chinese studied plants and their value in treating diseases and illnesses more than 5,000 years ago. Substances extracted from plants were the only source of medicines until the 19th century. Nowadays, nearly all drugs are made in laboratories. How do scientists develop and test a new drug?

Although most of the drugs used today are made in laboratories, many of them are actually pure forms of chemicals that were originally discovered in plants or animals. Once the active chemical is found, the medicine is made in the laboratory because it can be made in large quantities.

People once chewed the bark of the willow tree to relieve the pain and fever of an illness called malaria. Scientists investigated the bark. They extracted a variety of chemical compounds from it and discovered that one of them, salicylic acid, was the substance that had the effect on malaria. Pure salicylic acid is very harmful to the delicate lining of the stomach, but another chemical made from it, acetylsalicylic acid, is safer. We know it as aspirin, probably the most commonly taken drug in the world today.

When the painkilling properties of aspirin were discovered, scientists looked for other drugs that had the same effect. One of them was a chemical called phenacetin. It was widely used as a painkiller until doctors found that it damaged the kidneys. When phenacetin was swallowed, it

Scientists continue to investigate the natural world to find new chemicals that might be developed into medicines.

was broken down in the body into a series of chemicals. One of these chemicals, paraphenetidin, is the one that damages the kidneys. Another, acetaminophen, is the one that actually kills pain. Scientists solved the kidney problem by getting rid of the harmful chemicals and making acetaminophen itself.

However, acetaminophen has a serious drawback, too. It must be taken in the right dose. If too much is taken, it can damage the liver and the patient may die. A new type of acetaminophen with an extra chemical called methionine that prevents liver damage is now available. This is one way that medicines develop. If a chemical proves to be a useful medicine but it has a serious side effect, scientists try to change it so that it still has its useful effect, but the side effect is reduced or eliminated.

WHAT IS PAIN?

When any part of the body is damaged by an injury or illness, the damaged cells release chemicals called prostaglandins. They act on nearby nerves which send electrical signals to the brain. In the brain, these signals are interpreted as pain. The brain has its own natural painkillers, called endorphins, which can reduce pain by stopping the pain signals passing from one brain cell to another. Two people who suffer identical injuries may feel different levels of pain if their brains release different amounts of endorphins.

Most painkilling medicines work by blocking the production of prostaglandins. Aspirin works at the site of the injury, but acetaminophen works by stopping the brain reacting to the prostaglandins and so eases the sensation of pain. The most powerful painkillers, such as morphine, also work by acting directly on the brain. They stop the brain changing pain signals into the sensation of pain itself. Morphine is one of a group of drugs called narcotics which also cause drowsiness, unconsciousness, or even death if they are given in large enough amounts. They are only used by doctors to treat the worst pain.

A POWERFUL PAINKILLER

Morphine is one of the most powerful painkillers available today. But scientists have now found a chemical called epibatidine that is 200 times more powerful than morphine. They found it in a very unlikely place – the skin of a frog that lives in Ecuador, South America.

A rain forest frog like this one has provided the source of a valuable medicine. Will other rain forest animals help us to fight disease in the future?

This powerful painkiller was named after the tiny poison arrow frog (*epipedobates tricolor*) that provided it. Discoveries like this show how important it is to save all sorts of animal and plant species from extinction. If this little frog had been allowed to die out, scientists would never have found this extraordinary chemical. No one knows how many other important, perhaps lifesaving, chemicals there may be yet to discover in the world's fast-disappearing forests and jungles.

MAKING MEDICINES

Developing new medicines is extremely expensive. A drug company may have to spend more than $225 million on research and development before it sells the first package of tablets. It can take eight to ten years to identify the most promising substances. Out of 10,000 chemical compounds investigated, less than 50 may go forward to the next stage. It can take up to six years to study the compounds in detail and work out how to manufacture them in large quantities.

During the next seven years, the drugs will be tested on healthy human volunteers for the first time. Scientists check on how quickly the drug is absorbed by the body and how it breaks down in the body. They also look for any undesirable side effects. The correct dose is worked out at this stage, too. After 10 to 15 years of research, this is the first opportunity that scientists have to see if the drug really does what they think it should do. They then have to satisfy the authorities that the drug is safe. And finally, they have to persuade doctors to try it.

A pharmacist in a hospital makes up a prescription for a patient from the racks of drugs.

Drugs may be supplied as capsules, pills, creams, or liquids (right). Some medicines are applied in a patch that is stuck on the skin. (Below) A patch containing a drug to prevent seasickness.

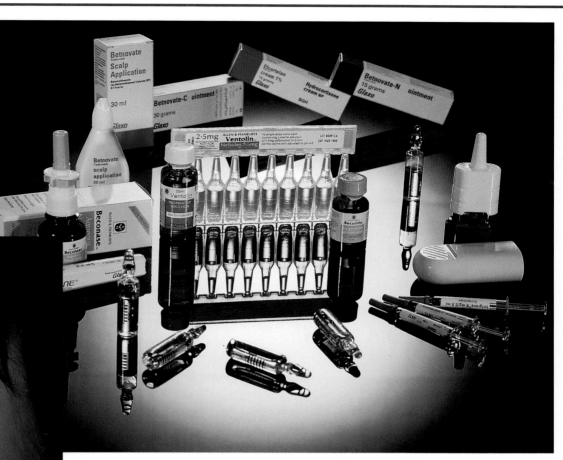

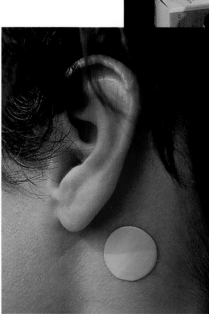

TAKING MEDICINES

To do its job effectively, a medicine has to get to the right part of the body. Some are rubbed on the skin. Others are dripped into the eyes or nose. But the most common way of taking a medicine is to swallow it in the form of tablets, pills, capsules, or a liquid. Once swallowed, it travels through the stomach to the small intestine. It passes through the wall of the intestine into the bloodstream and the blood carries it around the body. Not all medicines can be swallowed, because they would be broken down by the digestive juices in the stomach. Others would not pass through the wall of the intestine into the bloodstream. Luckily, there are other ways of getting these medicines into the body. They can be breathed in or injected, for example.

Medicines used to treat breathing difficulties like asthma may be inhaled, so that they reach the lining of the lungs instantly and help the sufferer to breathe more easily. An asthma sufferer's breathing difficulties are caused by muscles tightening around the tiny airways in the lungs, making them smaller. The lining of the airways swells up too, making them even smaller. An asthma sufferer can use a device called an inhaler to breathe in the medicine. It goes directly to the affected parts of the lungs, opening the airways to make breathing easier.

Some drugs can pass through the skin. A pad called a transdermal patch containing the medicine is stuck on the skin. The medicine then slowly dissolves through the skin.

THE POWERHOUSE

A weightlifter develops very big muscles with more "fast" fibers than most other athletes.

Weightlifters usually have bigger muscles than most people. Tennis players have well-developed muscles in their racket arm. How are scientists beginning to unravel the story of how muscles develop and why exercise makes them bigger? And how might this research hold the key to curing diseases like muscular dystrophy?

Muscles are able to contract and stretch again because they are made from fibers that can slide past each other, lengthening or shortening the muscle. The fibers are made from proteins, and genes control the production of the proteins. Scientists have found that genes vary the growth of muscles to suit the way the muscles are used. If a muscle is not exercised, it wastes (shrinks) because the genes have reduced the production of muscle protein.

There are three different types of muscle fibers. One can contract very quickly. The second is better at longer-lasting movements or movements that are repeated over and over again. The third type is a mixture of the first two. As long-distance runners train by going on long runs, they develop more of the slower, longer-lasting fibers in their legs. A sprinter's training develops more of the fast fibers. And that is why a long-distance runner cannot run

A muscle is made up of bundles of fine fibers, which in turn form groups of bundles. The whole muscle is contained in a tissue covering. Muscles concerned with voluntary movement have a fat middle and tapering ends (tendons) which are attached to a bone (see inset).

Sprinters develop more "fast" muscle fibers while long-distance runners develop more of the "slower" fibers.

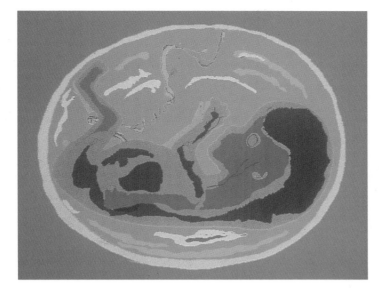

The limbs of this unborn baby are already clearly developed, at only 14 weeks old. Its muscles will continue to develop until birth, although it cannot move very much.

as fast over 330 feet as a sprinter, and a sprinter makes a poor marathon runner. Their muscles are made from different types of fibers.

BEFORE BIRTH

One question that has puzzled scientists is how a baby's muscles manage to grow before it is born. Floating in liquid inside its mother, it has no way of exercising its muscles. Mothers can often feel their unborn baby moving and kicking, but these movements are not enough to build muscles. Researchers have found that an unborn baby's muscles are made from a different protein from adult muscles. It may be that the baby's muscles do not need to exercise to grow. They may grow like the rest of the developing baby and change to adult-type muscles after birth.

If scientists can understand how genes control muscle growth, especially in babies, it may give them a way of reversing diseases, like muscular dystrophy, which make muscles waste away.

MUSCLE FUEL

If we make a repeated movement, like pedaling a bicycle, we find that the muscles we are using seem to lose their power after a while. They cannot keep going forever, because they run out of energy. Energy makes movement possible. A car cannot move without the energy

released by burning its fuel. Muscle fuel is a chemical called adenosine triphosphate, or ATP. If the supply of ATP dries up, the muscle stops working, like a car that has run out of gas. Fast muscle fibers use up ATP more quickly than it is supplied, so they get tired after a short time. Slow fibers use ATP at roughly the same rate as it is supplied, so they can keep going for longer.

Researchers have found that some other mammals have a fourth type of muscle. Cats, for example, have a special super-fast muscle in their jaw that enables them to bite very quickly – very useful for killing prey and repelling attackers. Perhaps further research among animals will help scientists in their battle against muscle-related diseases in people.

A tiger uses its special jaw muscles to tear at its prey.

THE TIRELESS PUMP

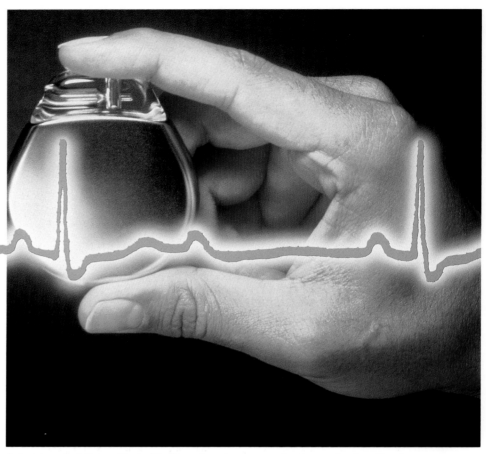

A heart pacemaker with, in the foreground, a computer trace of a heartbeat.

Heart disease is a major killer in many countries, especially in the western world. Until the 1960s, most people whose heart stopped could not be saved. Now, most can be revived. How have doctors learned how to keep a diseased heart going? And how do they bring people back from the brink of death from heart attacks?

The adult heart beats roughly 75 times every minute and if you multiply that by the number of minutes in the average lifetime, you will find that the heart has to beat 3 billion times. The heart is a muscle that "beats" by contracting to squeeze blood out through blood vessels to the body. Muscles usually get tired after a while and have to rest, but heart muscle is unique – fortunately for us it does not get tired!

Like any other organ in the body, the heart can go wrong. If the heart valves are faulty, they can be replaced by artificial valves. If the heart's blood vessels are narrowed, they can be opened up again by passing a tiny balloon into the vessel and blowing it up for a few moments.

Sometimes, the blood vessels that supply the heart may be so badly diseased that they cannot be saved. Doctors can take a vessel from somewhere else in the body

Eating too much fatty food can lead to heart disease.

One drug for treating heart disease, called digitalis, comes from the foxglove plant.

HEARTBEAT

If the heart stops beating, it is often possible to start it again. Everyone who takes a first aid course is taught how to restart someone's heart by pressing rhythmically on the patient's chest. If this does not work and if the necessary equipment is near at hand, doctors or nurses may give the heart an electrical shock. Electrical contacts are placed on the chest and a powerful electric pulse shoots between them. In many cases, this shock is enough to make the heart start beating again.

If a patient has a faulty heart, doctors may decide to open the chest and place a battery-powered device called a pacemaker inside to keep it beating regularly. The latest generation of pacemakers do not do anything unless they detect an abnormal heart rhythm. Some can even double as a machine to restart a heart, by sending out a strong electrical shock.

and use it to replace the diseased vessel.

Drugs can help, too, by making the heart beat more regularly, by reducing stress, reducing blood pressure, or widening narrow blood vessels so that blood flows more easily through them. A drug called digitalis found in the leaves of the foxglove plant slows the electrical signals that make the heart beat and therefore reduces the heart rate. A group of drugs called diuretics are used to reduce the amount of water in the blood by turning it into urine so that the heart has less blood to pump around. Another group of drugs called vasodilators are used to widen blood vessels that are too narrow. They work by neutralizing the chemical messengers in the blood that make the vessels narrower. This helps the heart because it does not have to beat with as much force to pump blood through wider vessels.

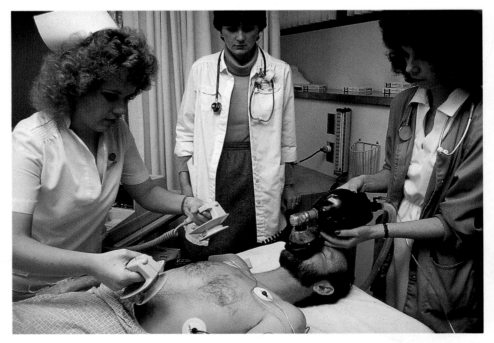

A patient is given an electrical shock to try to start his heart beating again.

HOW DOES THE HEART WORK?

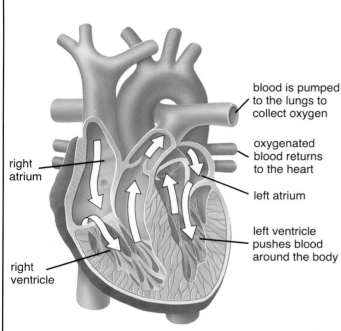

blood is pumped to the lungs to collect oxygen

oxygenated blood returns to the heart

left atrium

left ventricle pushes blood around the body

right atrium

right ventricle

The heart has four chambers – two atria at the top and two larger ventricles at the bottom. The atria receive blood and pass it on to the ventricles, which pump it out again. The right ventricle pumps blood to the lungs to collect oxygen. The blood returns to the left atrium. When this contracts, the blood is pushed down into the left ventricle. This is the thickest heart muscle because it has to be strong enough to push blood around the body. The blood returns to the right atrium. When this is full, it contracts and pushes blood down into the right ventricle, which sends the blood back to the lungs, and so on. Valves in the heart ensure that blood is always pumped in one direction. If it starts to be sucked back in the wrong direction, the flow snaps the valves shut.

BLOOD RELATIONS

An adult body has about ten and a half pints of blood in it. This red liquid is essential to life. It supplies the body's cells with the oxygen they need, takes away their waste materials, and distributes heat evenly around the body. But what is blood?

Blood contains three different types of cells – red cells, white cells, and platelets. Most of them are made in the bone marrow, the jellylike material in the middle of bones. Each cubic millimeter of blood contains roughly four and a half million red cells, 10,000 white cells and 200,000 platelets. The red cells contain hemoglobin, which absorbs oxygen from air in the lungs and carries it around the body. The white blood cells are part of the body's defense mechanism. As they circulate through the blood, they surround and devour microscopic organisms invading from the outside world.

A magnified view of bone marrow, showing developing red blood cells (in red).

Platelets are tiny particles that are essential for blocking leaks in blood vessels. All these cells are carried through the blood vessels by a straw-colored liquid called plasma. Plasma is 90 percent water, but it also contains vitamins, proteins, salts, hormones, and sugar.

One person's blood looks much the same as anyone else's, but in fact there are several types of blood with important differences between them. Some of them cannot be mixed together. If they *are* mixed, the cells clump together forming clots, which block blood vessels. The four main blood groups are called A, B, AB, and O. The ways in which they can and cannot be mixed are now well known.

People who live in the Himalayas and other mountainous regions are adapted to survive in air with less oxygen.

GIVING BLOOD

Blood is collected from blood donors and stored in plastic bags at a temperature of about 39°F. It normally has to be used within 3-4 weeks. Blood that is not used in this time is separated into its various parts. The liquid part, plasma, is dried to form a fine powder which can be kept indefinitely. It can be made into a liquid again by adding pure water. If someone loses a lot of blood, a plasma transfusion may be given to restore the blood pressure quickly. Once blood of the right type is available, a blood transfusion can be given.

BREEDING BLOOD CELLS

The higher up in the atmosphere you go, the thinner the air is and the more difficult it is to breathe. People who live in the higher regions of the world adapt to the conditions there by producing more red blood cells to absorb more oxygen from the air. In theory, it should be possible for athletes to train at high altitudes so that they, too, make more red blood cells. Then when they run in a race closer to sea level, their blood would be super-efficient at extracting oxygen from the air. The ideal way of doing this would be to live several thousand feet above sea level, but train and race at sea level. That is rather difficult to arrange, but there is a way of imitating these conditions to trick the body. The athlete sleeps inside a special chamber. Some of the air is pumped out to simulate the thinner air at a higher altitude. The body reacts to the low pressure by making more red blood cells. Then, in the daytime, the athlete trains as normal. The extra red cells supply the body with more oxygen, which enables the body to send more energy to the muscles.

HISTORY SPOTLIGHT

We know that the heart pumps blood around the body, but this was not actually proved until about 1650. When the English physician William Harvey studied animals, he found that the heart pumps blood to the lungs to collect oxygen. It then returns to the heart, from where it is pumped around the body through the arteries, returning to the heart through the veins. It was another 250 years before an Austrian scientist, Karl Landsteiner, discovered the four main blood groups that we still use today.

William Harvey demonstrating his theory of the circulation of blood to King Charles I of England.

THE BODY'S MESSENGERS

Electrical signals from the brain make the muscles work. Chemical signals control a wide range of activities including how tall we grow, how we store energy, and how much sugar we have in our blood. When this internal communications system is damaged or becomes faulty, can doctors repair it?

If you want to pick up a glass of water, you just reach out and pick it up. But how do you do it? This simple action turns out to be very complicated. It relies on messages traveling quickly to and from the brain. The messages that make this possible are electrical signals traveling along nerves.

HOW DO NERVES WORK?

A nerve cell looks like a long fiber with finely branched ends. Nerve cells meet at these branched endings, but they do not actually touch. There is a tiny gap called a synapse between them. When one cell is stimulated (turned on), an electric current travels along it to the end where it releases chemicals called neurotransmitters. These travel across the synapse to the next nerve cell. That makes the next cell fire and send an electric current along it. In this way, an electrical signal travels from nerve cell to nerve cell through the body. The fastest nerve signals travel at almost 174 miles per hour.

There are three types of nerve cells, or neurons. Sensory neurons carry information from the senses to the brain. Integrated neurons, or interneurons, process the information, and motor neurons carry instructions back from the brain to the muscles.

CHEMICAL MESSENGERS

The body has a second system for sending messages around the body which is entirely chemical. While nerves carry fast signals, chemical messages travel more slowly and have a longer-lasting effect. The messages are in the form of substances called hormones, which are

The central nervous system – the brain and spinal cord – is connected to the rest of the body by a network of nerve fibers called the peripheral nervous system. We can only control half of this system, the half that links our senses to the brain and the brain to our muscles. The other half is our "autopilot." It keeps our heart beating, makes sure we breathe even when we are asleep, and looks after our digestion and blood supply.

released from glands in various parts of the body. The whole system is called the endocrine system. If you are frightened, the feeling of "butterflies" in your stomach is caused by the hormone adrenaline released by the adrenal glands in your sides. It makes your heart beat more quickly and redirects blood from your stomach to the muscles, preparing you for "fight or flight."

Sex hormones (testosterone in men and estrogen in women) make a man's body develop differently from a woman's. The pancreas releases two other important hormones – insulin and glucagon. Insulin makes cells absorb glucose from the blood. Glucagon makes cells release glucose into the blood. It is important to keep the right level of glucose in our blood. The brain depends on glucose. It has no energy store itself so it draws on the supply of glucose to fuel it.

MAKING REPAIRS

The body's complex electrical and chemical control systems can go wrong because of disease or injury. Chemical problems can be put right quite easily by correcting the chemical balance. If the pancreas makes too little insulin, for example, the result is a condition called diabetes. Diabetics inject themselves with extra insulin every day to keep their blood sugar on an even keel. Damage to the body's electrical circuitry is more difficult to correct.

There is an important difference between the central and peripheral nervous systems. Peripheral nerves can repair themselves. Central nerves cannot. If you are unlucky enough to damage your spine, for example, the severed nerves will not grow together again and the activities controlled by nerves below the break will be lost forever.

Simpler animals, like leeches and frogs, are able to regrow their central nerves. Mammals like us actually produce a protein in our central nervous system that stops nerves from growing. So, even if a piece of leg nerve is transplanted into a damaged spine, it will not grow. Scientists are grappling with the problem of overriding this system and making damaged central nerves grow. If brain cells could be made to regrow, scientists might also be able to treat brain diseases, like Alzheimer's disease and Parkinson's disease.

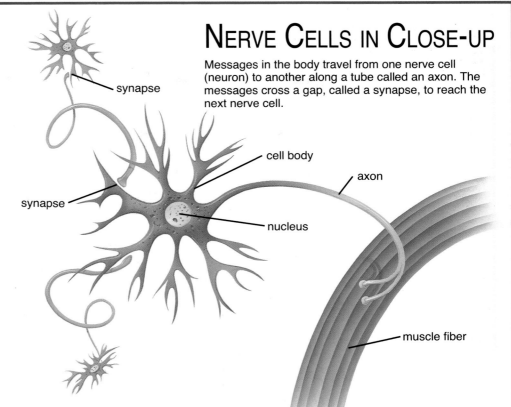

NERVE CELLS IN CLOSE-UP

Messages in the body travel from one nerve cell (neuron) to another along a tube called an axon. The messages cross a gap, called a synapse, to reach the next nerve cell.

synapse

synapse

cell body

axon

nucleus

muscle fiber

Dangerous activities may force the body to produce adrenaline.

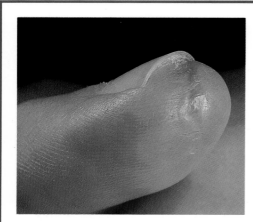

A cut finger, healing.

YOUR FLEXIBLE FRIEND

Skin is a remarkable material. It is tough, waterproof, and flexible. It grows as we grow and it is the body's first line of defense against infection. What is skin and how does it repair itself when it is damaged? And how can sunbathing prove fatal?

Skin is divided into two main layers. The part you can see is the epidermis. It is mostly made from dead cells that are continually being pushed up to the surface by new cells growing underneath. The dead cells are being shed all the time. In fact, most of the "dust" in your home is actually dead skin! Beneath the epidermis is the dermis, a living layer with a rich blood supply. Special cells buried in both layers sense touch, pressure, heat, cold. and pain. If you are too hot, sweat glands in the skin are stimulated to make a salty liquid which is carried up to the skin's surface. It evaporates, taking the energy it needs for evaporation from the body, which therefore cools down. If you are too cold, tiny muscles pull hairs on the skin upright, a condition often described as "goose flesh." This is common in the animal kingdom. If an animal fluffs out its fur, pockets of air are trapped next to the skin to help insulate the body. But we have so little body hair that the system does not do us much good.

A HEALTHY COLOR?

The skin contains cells called melanocytes that give it color by making a dark pigment (coloring) caled melanin. Very dark people and very fair people have the same numbers of melanocytes in their skin. Darker-skinned people are browner because their melanocytes make more melanin. People who live in the sunniest countries are usually dark-skinned because the extra melanin in their skin helps to protect them from the sun's rays.

Fair-skinned people who go out in the sun too much risk damaging their skin. At one time in the past, it was fashionable for people to have a very pale skin because it showed they were so wealthy that they did not have to go out to work on the land. They could spend all day relaxing indoors. They even dusted their skin with lead-based compounds to make it as pale as possible, not realizing that lead was poisonous. Nowadays, it is more fashionable for fair-skinned people to have a

These children on a beach in Australia are well protected against the fierce sun.

"healthy" tan. However, achieving today's fashionable look can be just as deadly as our ancestors' practice.

The ultraviolet radiation in sunlight that produces a tan can cause skin cancer (see page 8). As international travel has become increasingly popular, making it easier for people to have a vacation in the sun, skin cancer has increased too. Sunlight seems to turn off the skin's own defense mechanism that can normally destroy cancerous cells. If one particular part of the DNA (see page 42) in the skin's cells is damaged, the cell may begin to divide rapidly, forming a tumor (a ball of cancerous cells). It is very important, therefore, to use a sun block that stops ultraviolet radiation from penetrating the skin.

NEW SKIN

When skin is so badly damaged that it is unlikely to regrow, the damaged area is covered with a new sheet of skin taken from the patient's own body, usually the thigh. The new skin is "grafted" onto the injured area. Sometimes, someone can be so badly injured that there is not enough healthy skin left for grafting. In 1985, artificial skin was used for the first time. In October of that year, a man in Massachusetts was very badly burned on over 80 percent of his body. At the nearby Massachusetts Institute of Technology, a scientist (Ioannis Yannas) had developed an artificial skin made from fibers of collagen – taken from sharkskin – bonded (stuck) to a sugary material and covered with a layer of silicone rubber. Collagen is a ropelike material made from protein and found in most parts of the body holding tissue together. The collagen and sugar help healthy skin cells to grow and spread into the artificial skin. The silicone rubber keeps out infections and stops fluid from leaking out of the burned area.

After about three weeks, the silicone rubber layer is taken off. When the bandages are finally removed, two or three months after the skin was burned, new skin lies underneath. The artificial skin looks just like real skin except that it has no hair and it does not sweat.

Sharkskin has been used to create artificial skin for humans.

HISTORY SPOTLIGHT

Some people lack a vital substance called factor 8 that is essential to make blood cells clump together to form a clot. Without it, even minor cuts go on bleeding. The condition is called hemophilia. It is an inherited condition. It almost always affects male children, but it is always passed on by their mother. Several royal families have been affected by it. Some of Queen Victoria's children and Czar Nicholas II of Russia's children suffered from it. Factor 8 can be extracted from blood donated by people who do not suffer from hemophilia. In the past, this carried the risk of infecting people who received it with diseases like hepatitis or the virus that causes AIDS (see pages 8-9). Factor 8 is now made safely by genetic engineering (see pages 42-43).

Queen Victoria and some of her family.

23

Spare Part Surgery

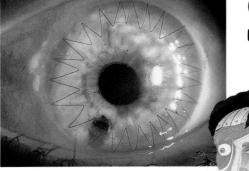

When a part or function of the body fails, doctors may be able to replace it, with a living or artificial part. How do transplants work? And how well can scientists imitate nature?

The cornea, a covering on the eye, can be replaced with one from someone who has died. Corneas can be kept chilled in an eye bank for up to a week. In this photograph, the new cornea is held in place with zigzag stiches.

Some parts of the body can be replaced with an artificial part. The parts that have been made successfully include skin, bone, joints, limbs, teeth, heart, blood, blood vessels, and parts of the eyes. But the body may reject an artificial part, although further attempts can be made to fit the new part since it does not deteriorate itself.

Most of the body is made from water, but it is not pure water. There are a lot of chemicals dissolved in it. When salt is dissolved in water it becomes very corrosive – it can eat into metals. Seawater is therefore very corrosive. The body is ten times more corrosive than seawater! Metals and plastics in the body are eaten into and broken down ten times more quickly than in seawater. As they break down, poisonous chemicals can be released into the body. Only the most corrosion-resistant materials can be used inside the body – metals like titanium and specially-designed plastics.

These are just some of the parts or functions of the body that can be replaced with artificial parts or donor organs. In the upper body they include skull plate, eyes, teeth, larynx, lungs, heart, heart valves and pacemakers, liver, kidneys, insulin pump, blood vessels, pancreas, muscle, shoulder and elbow joints, and lower arm.

In the lower body they include hip and knee joints, shin plates and lower legs. Skin for skin grafts is often taken from the legs.

Artificial hearts

Scientists have been trying to make artificial hearts since the 1950s, mainly in the United States. If an artificial heart could be made successfully, it would end the problem of a patient with a failing heart having to wait for a suitable natural heart to become available. The difficulty lies not in making the machine – scientists and engineers can make machines to work like most organs except the brain. The main difficulty they face is in making the machine small and light enough to fit inside the body and work reliably for many years.

The first artificial hearts given to people in the early 1980s were powered by an air pump outside the body. In the future, artificial hearts will have to be small, self-contained devices that can be placed inside the chest without the need for any large pieces of equipment outside the body. "Totally implantable" artificial hearts like this are being developed in the United States and Japan. However, these heart replacement operations are extremely costly. Many doctors believe that it would be better to teach people how to live a more healthy way of life so that in the future fewer people will need new hearts.

Dealing with lungs

The lining of the lungs is very delicate and easily damaged. If the air is full of sharp particles or fibers, they can scrape and scar the lining, making it more difficult for oxygen to pass through. A material called asbestos used to be widely used in buildings and household appliances because it was tough and fireproof. People who made asbestos or breathed air full of asbestos fibers often developed an illness that left them very short of breath. It became known as asbestosis because it was due to the harmful effects of the asbestos fibers. Miners can suffer from a similar illness called silicosis, caused by breathing in rocky particles of silica. Damaged lungs can sometimes be replaced with real lungs from a donor who has just died. The heart is often replaced at the same time as the lungs in a heart-lung transplant operation.

Robot doctors

Computers and robots are being developed to help surgeons operate, especially where very fine movements are needed.

A robot system developed for eye operations helps surgeons to manipulate their instruments more accurately than ever. The surgeon moves a set of controls linked to a computer. The computer then operates a set of instruments. When the surgeon moves a control, the computer moves an instrument, but the instrument moves as little as one thousandth as far as the control. This enables the surgeon to move the instruments with far greater precision than a pair of

A worker wears a protective suit and breathing mask while handling sacks of asbestos fiber waste.

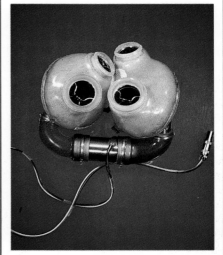

HISTORY SPOTLIGHT

The first person to be given an artificial heart was an American doctor. The operation began on December 1, 1982 at the Utah Medical Center in Salt Lake City and ended the next day. The surgeon implanted a Jarvik-7 heart in the patient's chest. Dr. Barney Clark lived for 112 days.

Jarvik-7, an artificial heart that had to be linked to equipment outside the body.

human hands working on their own, and without any shaking.

Because a computer operates the instruments, the surgeon need not be in the same room as the patient. The controls operated by the surgeon can be installed in another room in the hospital, linked to the computer and instruments by cable. In fact, the surgeon could be thousands of miles away, linked to the computer by satellite. Television cameras give the surgeon a clear view of the operation and what the instruments are doing.

Robots have already helped some surgeons to perform hip replacement operations. When a hip joint becomes diseased and so painful that its owner cannot walk any more, doctors may decide to replace it with an artificial hip joint. In 1992, Californian surgeons left the tricky operation of drilling into the patient's bone to a robot. The same system will probably be used for fitting artificial knees.

SIDE EFFECTS

The body's ability to recognize which cells are its own and which are not is vital. Without it, disease-causing organisms could invade the body and spread unchecked. The slightest infection could be fatal. But when the first transplants (organ swaps) were attempted, doctors had to find a way of stopping the immune system from attacking the new organ. They started by using drugs that stopped the immune system from working. That stopped the body from rejecting the new organ, but it also left the body defenseless against other infections. Drugs used to fight cancer have been tried, but they also cut the production of red blood cells. If the number of red blood cells is reduced too much, it can cause a condition called anemia. Other drugs can cause high blood pressure, damage the stomach lining, or damage the kidneys. Another solution was needed.

TRYING A DIFFERENT APPROACH

All the attempts to fight organ rejection with drugs seem to have serious side effects, so researchers are now trying a different approach. They are experimenting with the thymus gland that controls the immune system. They are trying to trick the thymus gland into believing that the transplanted organ belongs to the body. The thymus produces white blood cells called T lymphocytes that attack foreign cells. Scientists have taken T cells from the donor body and injected them into the thymus gland of the body that will receive the new organ. They have found that the new organ survived for much longer and the body's immune system carried on working normally. So far, all the experiments with T cells have been carried out on rats and mice, but the researchers think that the technique should also work in humans. In the future, someone receiving a new heart, kidney, or liver might also be given an injection of the donor's T cells into their thymus gland to stop the immune system from attacking the new organ.

(Opposite) An operating room during heart surgery.

The first heart transplant was performed on December 3, 1967 at the Groote Schuur Hospital in Cape Town, South Africa. The operation on the 55-year-old patient, Louis Washkansky, lasted five hours. It was performed by a team of 30 people headed by Professor Christiaan Barnard. Mr. Washkansky lived for only 18 days. As doctors have learned more about transplanting organs, they have become more successful and their patients have lived longer. The longest surviving heart transplant patient lived for nearly 23 years after he received his new heart.

Professor Christiaan Barnard with a patient.

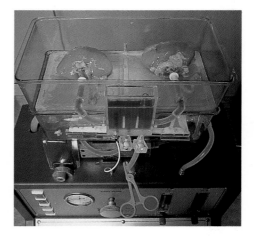

Donor kidneys can be chilled for a short time until they are used in a transplant operation.

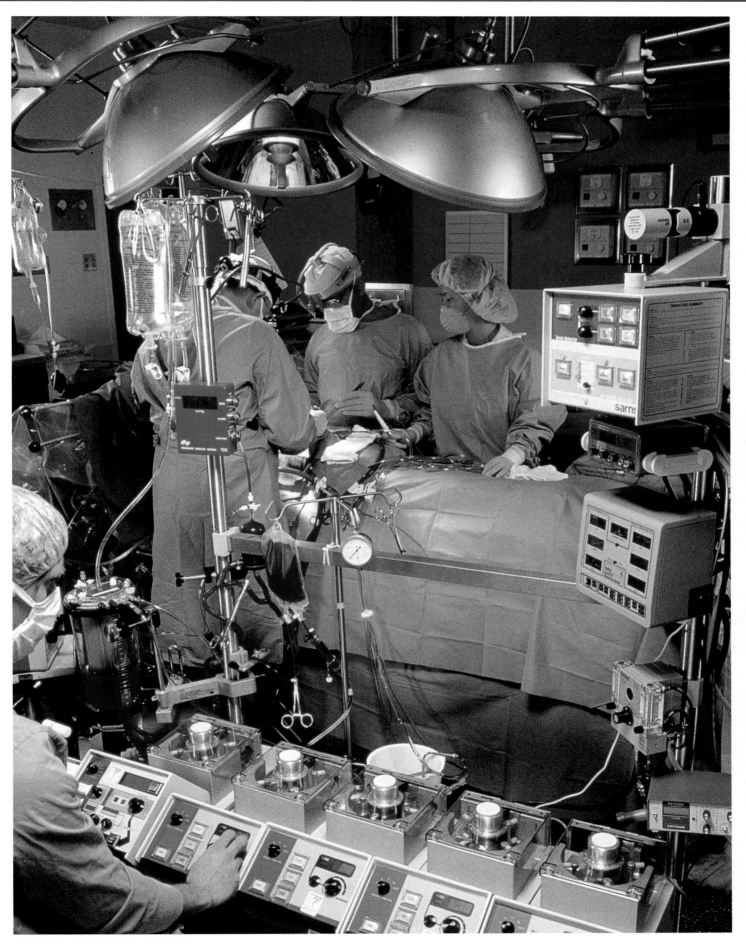

LOOKING INSIDE THE BODY

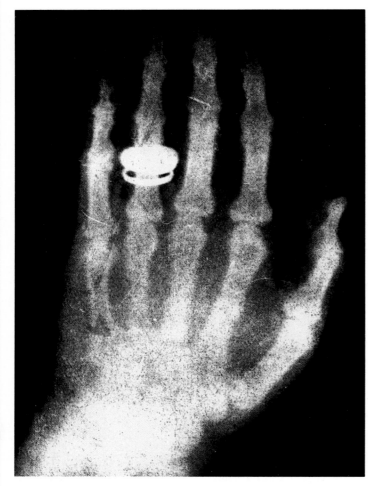

The first X-ray photograph was made in 1896. It shows the inventor's wife's hand and her ring.

A CAT scan of a man's chest. The left-hand lung is healthy. The one on the right is cancerous.

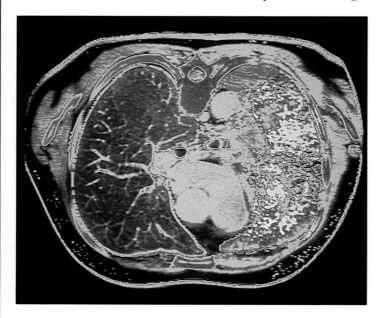

Oone hundred years ago, people were astounded by the discovery that strange rays that became known as X rays could pass painlessly through the human body and strike a photographic plate, making a picture of the body's internal structures. Doctors still use X rays to look for breaks in bones and the telltale signs of an infection or a tumor. But now there are much more advanced imaging techniques that can tell doctors a great deal more than a simple X ray.

By combining an X-ray machine with the information processing power of a computer, it is possible to produce pictures that could not normally be taken. A computerized axial tomography scanner (CAT scanner) produces pictures of slices through the body. It works by rotating an X-ray source around the patient and measuring the strength of the X rays picked up after they have passed through the body. The computer then combines all the information and constructs the image of what a slice through the body would look like.

PICTURES VIA MAGNETS

A second body scanning technique uses the fact that hydrogen atoms in the body are affected by magnetic fields in a way that can be measured. When the patient's body is bathed in a strong magnetic field, its hydrogen atoms swing round to lie in the same direction as the magnetic field. Pulses of radio waves momentarily knock the atoms out of alignment. When they swing back to lie along the magnetic field again, they produce a signal of their own that can be measured and used to produce a picture.

Magnetic Resonance Imaging (MRI) scanning

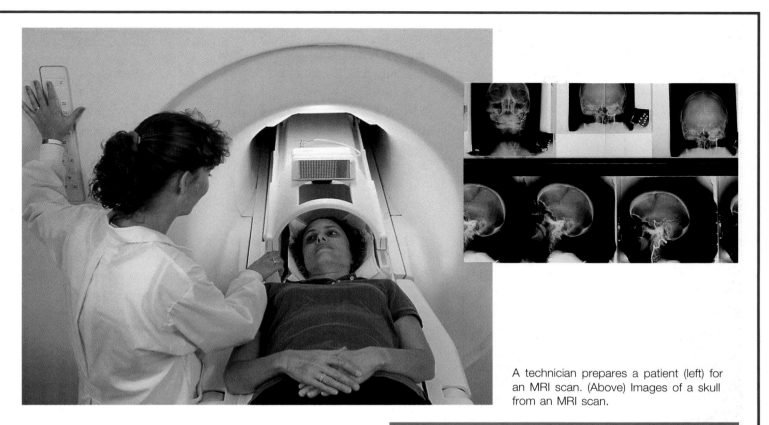

A technician prepares a patient (left) for an MRI scan. (Above) Images of a skull from an MRI scan.

has two main advantages over CAT scanning. First, it does not use X rays, which can be harmful to the body. Second, it can show up differences between soft tissues that X rays cannot show.

A PET SCANNER

Just before a patient has a PET scan (positron emission tomography scan), he or she is injected in the arm with a mildly radioactive form of glucose. After a few moments, the blood carries this into the brain. The patient lies with his or her head inside a circle of radiation detectors which detect particles flying out from the radioactive glucose in the brain. A computer traces the paths of the particles to find out which part of the brain they came from. The glucose becomes more concentrated in the parts of the brain that are working most actively. The computer produces a colored picture of a slice through the brain, where the colors represent different levels of activity. After the scan, the glucose loses its radioactivity very quickly. Certain conditions, such as Alzheimer's disease, schizophrenia, and a form of depression, called manic depression, produce distinctive PET scans that look very different from a normal brain scan.

HISTORY SPOTLIGHT

The story of medical imaging began with Wilhelm Röntgen in 1895. Röntgen was studying how electricity traveled through a gas inside a cathode ray tube (similar to a television picture tube). Röntgen noticed that the gas in the tube was glowing, something that other researchers had seen, but he also noticed a nearby screen was glowing too. Invisible rays from the tube seemed to be affecting it. Röntgen studied these rays and found that they could pass through a variety of materials and also darken a photographic plate. The medical importance of the discovery was quickly realized. The rays could pass through the human body and make a shadow picture of the bones on a photographic plate. Röntgen received the first Nobel Prize for Physics in 1901 for his work.

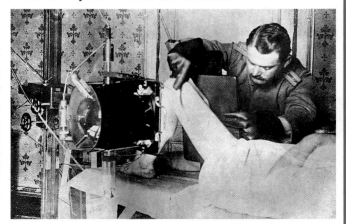

Röntgen's X-ray discovery was used in Germany in World War I.

SURGERY WITHOUT CUTTING

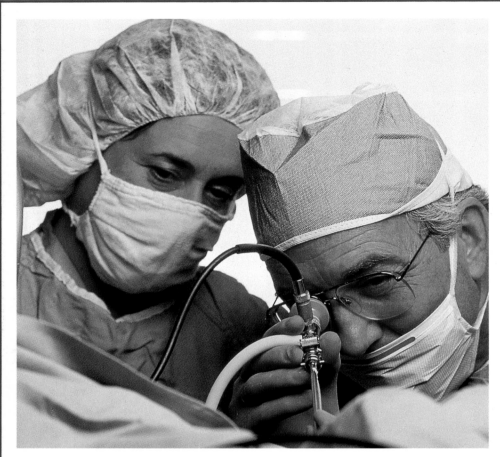

A surgeon using an endoscope to see inside a patient's body without major surgery.

Surgical operations always used to involve cutting a patient open so that surgeons could remove or repair a part of the body. Now, doctors are developing new treatments that can be carried out without opening the body.

In the past, when doctors were not sure what exactly a patient's problem was or precisely where it was, they might carry out an exploratory operation. Nowadays, instead of this major operation, doctors have a range of techniques to form pictures of the body's interior (see pages 28-29). They can also use small probes to look inside the body. The probe can be inserted into the body through the mouth to examine the throat, stomach, or lungs, or through a small nick in the skin to examine the internal organs. A light at the tip of the probe illuminates the patient's interior and enables the surgeon to see clearly through an eyepiece. Some operations are carried out by using blood vessels as pipes or ducts to guide instruments through the body.

THE LIGHT FANTASTIC

Lasers play an important part in modern surgery, especially in eye operations and some cancer treatments. The retina, the light-sensitive layer of the eye, is attached to the back of the eyeball, on the inside. But it sometimes peels away from the back wall of the eyeball. Nowadays, the retina can be reattached in place, using a laser. The laser beam is shone through the pupil and focused onto the retina. It heats a tiny spot of the retina enough to attach it to the cells of the eyeball behind it.

Cancerous cells can be killed by using a powerful laser that vaporizes any cells the beam strikes, provided they are on or near the surface. But lasers cannot penetrate deep into opaque tissue.

By using lasers, doctors can operate on the eye without making cuts.

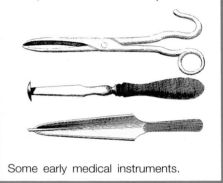
SHOCK WAVES

Ultrasound can be used to treat painful kidney stones. The stones are formed by excess salts in the urine or an infection that forms crystals in the urine which build up over time to form a hard stone. Bursts of ultrasound focused on the stones produce shock waves that shatter them. The treatment continues until the stones have been pulverized into pieces that are small enough to pass out of the body naturally in the urine.

NANOTECHNOLOGY

In the future, tiny machines might be injected into the body to repair some problems instead of opening it up to operate from the outside. Tiny rotating cutters could circulate in the blood, scraping away the clogged-up lining of diseased blood vessels. Other tiny instruments – micro-pipettes – could be used to fertilize human eggs with sperm, to help infertile couples. Engineers and doctors have developed micro-pipettes so small that each is only one fiftieth the width of a human hair. Until now, these miniature tools have been used to handle pollen grains and moon dust. These developments are part of a new science known as nanotechnology, which is named after the Greek word *nanos*, meaning dwarf. To modern scientists, nano means one billionth. For example, a nanometer is a billionth of a meter or a millionth of a millimeter.

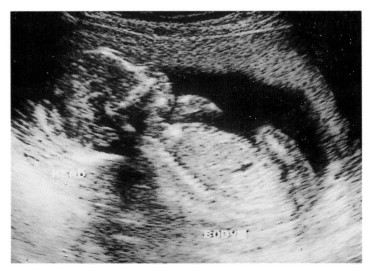

Ultrasound has been used to monitor unborn babies (left) since the 1950s. Now it can also be used to treat kidney stones without cutting open the patient's body.

ALL IN THE MIND

The brain controls everything that we do. It is such a complex organ that it is not surprising that it sometimes develops faults. It is protected by unique defenses against organisms that might harm it but some do get through. Scientists are trying to mimic these organisms in order to get medicines into the brain.

Each side of the brain consists of four main lobes. The front lobes are concerned with our thoughts and emotions. The other lobes control our senses. The cerebellum, at the base of the brain, controls balance and coordination.

It may be possible to treat tap water to reduce the risk of Alzheimer's disease.

UNLOCKING THE BLOOD-BRAIN DOOR

Medical problems in the brain are particularly difficult to treat because the brain tries to keep out everything (including medicines) that might harm it. Only the simplest substances that it needs for its survival are allowed in. Most of the body's blood vessels have leaky walls that let chemicals, gases, liquids, and some organisms through. The walls of the brain's blood vessels let almost nothing through. Most bacteria do not affect the brain because they cannot get through this "blood-brain barrier," but one disease, meningitis, does get through. Researchers found that meningitis bacteria are somehow able to get through the blood-brain barrier and infect the watery fluid that cushions the brain.

Researchers believe that part of the bacteria's cell wall works like a chemical key, unlocking the door to let them through the blood-brain barrier. If scientists can copy this key and add it to drugs, they would have a way of getting drugs directly into the brain. They are studying this possibility by separating bacterial cell walls into all the various substances from which they are made. Each is injected separately into the bloodstream. Then a chemical that can be traced (perhaps because it is radioactive) is injected into the body. If this is detected in the brain, the scientists know that the blood-brain barrier has been opened safely. If the research is successful, it will open the way to a new generation of treatments for brain disorders.

ALZHEIMER'S DISEASE

People live longer nowadays because of better diet, healthier life-styles, and improved medical care. As a result, more people are suffering from diseases associated with old age. One of them,

Alzheimer's disease, is now the most common reason for mental decline in old age. Sufferers gradually lose their memory and then their ability to do more and more activities as their brain cells shrink and die. Researchers believe that the disease is due to a build-up of a substance called amyloid protein, which seems to damage brain cells. When scientists understand what controls the amyloid levels in the brain, they may be able to prevent Alzheimer's disease by reducing amyloid production in the body or by making the brain extra-efficient at clearing it away.

There may be a link between aluminum and Alzheimer's disease. Some people absorb more aluminum, from food and drink, than others, and it has been found in the brains of patients who have died. Researchers have found that silicon, another element found in the ground, can reduce the amount of aluminum absorbed by the body. Scientists are investigating the possibility of adding silicon to drinking water supplies to reduce the risk of Alzheimer's disease.

MIND OVER MATTER

The power of the mind over the body is undoubted. If you concentrate on staying calm and quiet, you can slow down your heart rate. Some people believe that the mind can heal the body. They believe they can cure some illnesses by turning the healing power of the mind inward on the body. Athletes often use the power of the mind in their sports to help them succeed. Sports psychology is now an important part of training and participating in events.

Yoga uses physical and mental exercises to improve a person's well-being.

ALTERNATIVE MEDICINE

Almost all modern medicines and treatments have undesirable side effects and risks. Surgical operations involve some risk, too. Usually, the benefits of the drug or operation greatly outweigh the risks. But as people become better informed about the risks and side effects, they are increasingly looking for other ways of dealing with their health problems.

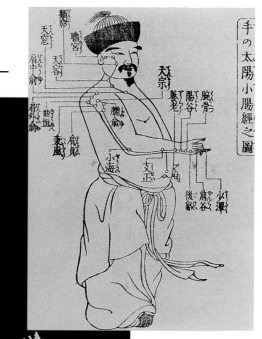

A 19th-century Japanese woodcut (above) shows some acupuncture points. Needles are inserted at these points (left) to relieve pain and illness.

ACUPUNCTURE

The Chinese have used acupuncture for at least 4,500 years. Acupuncture is based on the belief that illness is the result of the body's energy balance being upset. An acupuncturist inserts fine needles into points of the patient's body that are said to lie over energy lines. Rotating the needles unblocks the energy lines, allows the energy to flow correctly around the body, and returns the body to a balanced healthy state. In a modern development of this, small electrical currents are passed through the needles to improve the effect.

HYPNOSIS

The use of trances and "waking sleep" states was very common in early civilizations. They were used in healing rituals and religious ceremonies. Modern hypnosis began with the Austrian physicist, Franz Mesmer. His ability to put people into a trance in the 18th century became known as mesmerism. His claims that illnesses could be cured by this method were investigated and rejected in 1784. However, by the 1820s, dentists and doctors were still using the technique to put patients to sleep for minor operations. By the 1880s, hypnosis (the new name for mesmerism) was assessed once again by doctors, but they could not agree on its value. It was finally accepted as a useful technique by the medical profession in 1955 in Britain and in 1958 in the United States.

Hypnosis seems to work by changing the mind into a different state from its normal wakefulness. And this altered state of mind can produce real physical changes in the body which can be measured. In this state, the mind is very receptive to suggestions made by the hypnotist. Hypnosis is now used for helping people end their addictions to drugs or alcohol, as an anesthetic to give pain relief during some operations, and to help people suffering from problems caused by stress and worry.

HOMEOPATHY

Conventional western medicine treats illnesses with "opposites," substances that act against the symptoms of the illness. Homeopaths, people who practice homeopathy, treat illnesses with "similars," substances that produce the same symptoms as the illness in a healthy person. But the substance is sometimes diluted so much that little of the original substance can be left in the mixture. This worries many people who wonder how the mixture can have any effect at all if so little of the active substance is left in it. Nevertheless, homeopathy is accepted as a useful and successful technique by many of the medical authorities that regulate and license medical practices around the world.

A mesmerist at work in the 19th century.

Other types of alternative medicine that are either already in widespread use or are being investigated include herbalism (the use of plants), acupressure (the use of rubbing and pressing on parts of the body), and aromatherapy (the use of plant oils, which are rubbed on the skin or breathed in).

Extracts from flowers, fruits, tree barks, and fungi are all used in alternative medicine.

Homeopathy was the result of one doctor's unhappiness with the medical practices of the 18th century. Then, doctors treated illnesses by methods that included bloodletting (draining blood from their patients, often by means of bloodsucking leeches) and purgation (flushing everything out of the stomach and intestines). The German doctor Samuel Hahnemann read about medicines like quinine that would produce the symptoms of a disease like malaria in a healthy person as well as curing it in a person who suffered from the disease. Hahnemann discovered more substances that produced the effects of certain illnesses in people. He diluted them in alcohol until the poisonous effects disappeared, but found that their ability to cure the same illnesses actually increased.

Leeches were once used to suck a patient's blood.

LIFE-STYLES

The first human beings hunted animals and gathered wild fruits. Their way of life meant that they had regular exercise and a varied diet. Today, many people's life-style is not so healthy.

A healthy way of life contains the same basic elements that made up our early ancestors' lives – exercise and a varied diet. Regular exercise does the body good in three ways. It improves stamina – the ability to keep going. It improves strength by building muscles. And it makes the body more supple (flexible). If the body is not exercised enough, we may not use up all the energy in the food we eat and the excess is stored as fat. The body can also stiffen up, making us more liable to suffer aches and pains. Regular exercise also helps to reduce the risk of heart disease.

For some people, walking to school or work and playing a sport regularly is enough. Others who drive everywhere, sit down at work, and watch television in the evening, can improve their health by taking a brisk 20-minute walk three or four times a week.

A HEALTHY DIET?

A well-balanced diet contains three main types of ingredients – fats, proteins, and carbohydrates. Sugars and starches are carbohydrates. The body changes them into a form of sugar called glucose and uses it for energy. Fats, obtained from eggs, nuts, cakes, butter, margarine, milk, and fatty meats, are a more concentrated form of energy. Too much of them literally makes us fat. Proteins, from milk, meat, cereals, and nuts, are essential for growth. They are broken down by the body into simpler substances called amino acids, which are then built up into new proteins to make new cells.

Many people in developed countries do not have enough exercise.

Fresh fruit and vegetables are an essential part of a healthy diet. They provide vitamins, minerals, and fiber.

HEART DISEASE

Fat deserves a special mention. Not all fat is the same. One type is more dangerous than the others because it can lead to heart disease. There are three types of fat: saturated, mono-unsaturated, and polyunsaturated. Eating foods with too much saturated fat can increase the amount of cholesterol that circulates in the blood. It is true that the body makes its own cholesterol, but a diet with too much saturated fat can increase this to dangerous levels that make a heart attack more likely. Foods high in polyunsaturates and low in saturates are therefore healthier.

Genes are also linked to heart disease (see pages 42-43). They make the proteins that carry cholesterol safely to the liver to be broken down. Several proteins can do the job, but some are better at it than others. The proteins we each have are made by genes. A person's chances of having a heart attack are therefore linked to the cholesterol-processing genes they inherit from their parents as well as to their diet and life-style.

HEALTH HAZARDS

Many people damage their health by drinking too much alcohol, smoking tobacco, or taking dangerous drugs. Alcohol is absorbed quickly by the body. In small amounts, it can make people feel relaxed and friendly, but too much can make people aggressive and violent. It also slows people's reactions. Drinking too much alcohol over a long period can cause liver damage and increase the drinker's risk of developing some cancers.

Cigarette smoking is very dangerous because it can cause lung cancer. People who smoke risk their own health, but they can also risk the health of other people. A pregnant woman who smokes is likely to have a baby that is smaller than average. People who work or live close to smokers may also be at risk of ill health because they breathe in the smoke breathed out by the smoker. This "passive smoking" is seen as such a risk that smoking is increasingly being banned from workplaces and even many public places.

Almost all of us take drugs at some time. Most of us take them in carefully controlled doses bought from a pharmacist or prescribed by a doctor. But some people choose to eat, inhale, or inject drugs that are extremely dangerous. The drug itself may be contaminated with anything from brick dust to poisonous chemicals. People who inject drugs and share the same needle also run the risk of passing dangerous diseases like hepatitis and AIDS between one another (see page 8). Drug abuse is a serious problem in many countries.

THE DEVELOPING WORLD

People living in the developing world do not enjoy the same freedom of choice in diet and life-styles as people in the wealthier countries. What can be done to improve poor hygiene and health care so that more and more people are able to live a healthy life?

In developing countries poverty is a major killer. Even in the relatively wealthy western countries, people living in poorer areas suffer worse health and do not live as long on the average as their wealthier citizens. In the developing world, poverty exacts an even higher price. The disease and illnesses associated with old age, eating refined foods, or the stresses and strains of living in the

Rice is the staple diet in many parts of the developing world. A diet based mostly on rice is not as healthy as the varied diets available in the rich, developed countries.

Slums in Manaus, Brazil. More than two thirds of the world's population live in the poorer developing countries.

developed world do not generally occur in developing countries. Infectious diseases and malnutrition are more serious.

People who live in the poorest developing countries often do not have enough to eat or lack a balanced diet. Many live in unhygienic conditions and have little or no access to medical care. The problems caused by poverty are often compounded by war, famine, or drought. Where there is water, it may be polluted with chemicals or organisms that carry diseases such as cholera. Water-borne diseases like cholera have been eliminated in the developed world by the systems that pipe clean water in and take dirty water away. Contaminated water can also carry the worms that cause a disease called "river blindness." In Africa, 18 million people suffer from river blindness.

There are drugs and chemical sprays that could be used to treat these diseases and to kill the pests that carry them, but many developing countries cannot afford to buy them in sufficient quantities to treat everyone. Even when drugs and sprays are available, improper use may allow some of the disease organisms or pests to survive and become resistant to further doses of the drugs or sprays. The wars that ravage certain developing countries often interrupt effective pest control programs. The genetic code of the pest can change too and may become resistant to existing chemical treatments. New drug-resistant forms of tuberculosis, cholera, and malaria are spreading rapidly in developing countries.

One way of reducing the incidence of disease is to provide a clean water supply and keep it completely separate from polluted waste water. In the developed countries water is cleaned by treating it with chlorine or a similar chemical that kills any living organisms in it. Water in third world countries is often taken from untreated streams and wells, but it can be made safe by boiling it before it is used for drinking. Education is vital too. If people understand what causes disease, how to recognize the early signs of diseases so that they can be treated in time and, for example, how to manage their land so that their crops do better, they can improve their own chances of survival. There may not be enough doctors to serve every village over a huge area, but in some countries selected local villagers are trained to go around

A village pump in Ghana. Projects to provide clean drinking water in third world countries are a vital part of the aid given by the richer, developed countries.

and teach people the basics of hygiene and health care. Outside aid may still be necessary – to sink boreholes to bring water to the surface or to supply food or medicines in emergencies, for example. But the best aid is in the form of education and programs that local people can operate and maintain themselves without the need for expensive foreign technology.

If there were fewer people, the existing water, food, and medical services would go further. Families in developing countries tend to be large. Where there are no "social services" to look after the ill and very old, and where children often die before they reach adulthood, people have large

A malaria clinic (above) in Cameroon. The disease is common in many developing countries and is spread by mosquitoes (right).

families so that enough children will survive to look after their parents. By using modern family planning methods, the average size of families in the third world has been cut from six people in the 1960s to four in the early 1990s.

People's activities can worsen disease problems, sometimes in surprising ways. Forest clearance can change the habitat of an insect or snail that carries a disease and let the disease spread into new areas where the people have no resistance to the disease. Scientists are beginning to learn more about how the distribution of disease-carrying mosquitoes and blackflies is changing in southeast Asia, Africa, and South America because of people's activities. For example, in Africa flies that normally live in

A health worker talking to mothers in Bangladesh about diet, illness, and family planning.

savanna (flat grassland) habitats are moving into new areas where the forest has been cleared and spreading the diseases they carry to the people who live and work there. In Brazil, mining, forest clearance, and road construction in what was tropical rain forest create numerous pools of water where malaria-carrying mosquitoes can breed. In Thailand, rubber and coffee plantations may provide a home for one form of malaria-carrying mosquito and this may account for at least some of the increase in malaria in parts of the country. Scientists are continually updating their understanding of how diseases are spread in developing countries and how they can be treated.

HISTORY SPOTLIGHT

Cholera was commonplace in Europe until the 19th century because no one really understood what caused it. In 1854, there was an outbreak of cholera in London, the third serious outbreak in just a few years. At that time, water was not piped into the houses of the poor. They had to collect water from handpumps in the street. Dr. John Snow thought that cholera might be spread by contaminated water, so he carried out an experiment. He took away the handle of a public water pump in Broad Street. The death rate fell. In fact, a cracked cesspool (an underground sewage tank) only a yard away was allowing sewage to flow into the drinking water supply. Snow's experiment proved that cholera was spread by polluted water.

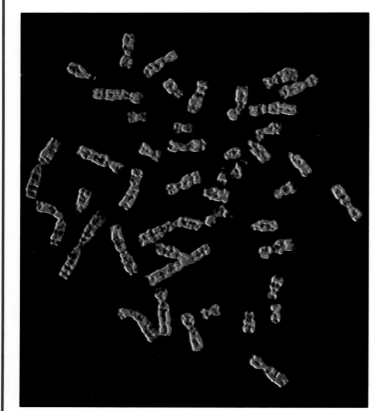

READING THE GENETIC CODE

We all grow and develop according to a set of instructions called the genetic code that tells our cells what to do. As scientists investigated this code, they found that it controlled not only how we grow and develop but also what illnesses we might suffer from, sometimes decades later. Genetics has become one of this century's most important branches of medical science. How is it unlocking the mysteries of our body?

Every human cell contains 23 pairs of chromosomes (above). The chromosomes carry the genetic information that tells our cells what to do.

The instructions that tell our cells how to grow and multiply are carried by genes made from long strands of DNA (deoxyribonucleic acid). The DNA is formed from two intertwined coils of molecules that look a bit like a spiral staircase. When a cell divides, each double spiral of DNA inside the cell unzips down the middle and splits in two. The two new cells formed from the division each contains one half of the DNA. This grows a second half to become a complete double spiral again. If all that DNA in each cell was uncoiled, it would measure about six and a half feet long. Multiply that by about 12 billion cells in the body and the DNA that each of us carries around inside our cells would circle the planet Earth 600 times, a distance of approximately 14.4 million miles!

ILLNESS AND GENES

A scientist studies a gel containing fragments of DNA under an ultraviolet light.

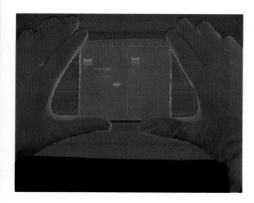

Some of us are more likely to suffer from certain illnesses and diseases because of our genetic makeup. Some cancers (uncontrolled cell division), heart disease, Huntingdon's disease, Down's Syndrome, Alzheimer's disease, cystic fibrosis, and many others seem to be linked to genes. Even illnesses that seem to have more to do with the sufferer's personality, like alcoholism, are proving to have genetic links. That does not mean that everyone who shares the same genetic code as people who suffer from an illness will develop the same illness. Very often, the genes that lead to the illness have to be triggered by another event before the person will develop the illness. The extra event might be damage to the cells by radiation or by infection, or high levels of stress. Scientists are just beginning to learn how these factors work together to produce illness.

GENETIC ENGINEERING

Knowing which genes do what and how they go wrong gives scientists a clue to how to correct the faults that cause genetic disorders. Faulty cells are not repaired. Instead, genes that make the proteins the body needs are added. As they divide, they make more healthy cells, all making the right proteins. Another approach is to use genetically-engineered bacteria as factories to make human proteins in enormous quantities, which can then be given to people who lack them. If scientists knew where all the genes were located on the chromosomes, which genes made which proteins, and which proteins were involved in which illnesses, they would have a chance of correcting many more genetic faults.

In the 1980s scientists embarked on an ambitious international project called the Human Genome Project to draw up a map of all the genes on every human chromosome. As more and more genes and their functions are discovered, there are breakthroughs in how genes and certain illnesses are linked. These new techniques of gene therapy will be used more and more to cure diseases and illnesses in the 21st century.

Fruit flies like this one are often used for basic genetic research because they have a simple genetic code and they multiply very rapidly.

GLOSSARY

Artery a blood vessel that carries blood away from the heart.

Bacteria living creatures from about .0004 of an inch across, responsible for diseases including typhoid, diphtheria, tetanus, and food poisoning.

Cell the basic building block of the body. Cells are specialized to do different jobs – some become muscles, others become nerves, skin, bone, and so on.

Chromosomes rod-shaped objects inside a cell's nucleus that contain the genes. Each gene controls one inherited characteristic.

DNA deoxyribonucleic acid, the genetic code. DNA is a long chain molecule resembling a twisted ladder. The rungs of the ladder are made from four types of links. The order of these links determines what the cell does.

Genetic engineering the manipulation of a person's genetic code to, for example, correct an inherited illness.

Germ a microorganism, including bacteria and viruses, that can cause a disease.

Radiation therapy the treatment of illnesses, especially cancer, with radiation that kills cells.

Transplant to replace a damaged or diseased organ with a new organ donated by someone else.

Vaccination giving someone a weakened form of a germ to give them immunity to an infection by the full-strength germs.

Vein a blood vessel that carries blood toward the heart.

Viruses the smallest known living creatures. Viruses cannot thrive or reproduce on their own. They use genetic material inside other cells to make copies of themselves. Viruses cause diseases including influenza (flu), measles, chicken pox, and polio.

Vitamins compounds which the body needs but cannot make for itself. Vitamins are an essential part of a healthy diet.

FURTHER READING

Aaseng, Nathan. *The Disease Fighters: The Nobel Prize in Medicine.* Lerner, 1987
Beckelman, Laurie. *Alzheimer's Disease.* Macmillan, 1990
Bender, Lionel. *Frontiers of Medicine.* Franklin Watts, 1991
Brown, Fern G. *Hereditary Disease.* Franklin Watts, 1987
Brownstone, David M. and Franck, Irene M. *Healers.* Facts on File, 1989
Burge, Michael C. *Vaccines: Preventing Disease.* Lucent Books, 1992
Check, William A. *The Mind-Body Connection.* Chelsea House, 1990
Durrett, Deanne. *Organ Transplants.* Lucent Books, 1993
Eagles, Douglas A. *Nutritional Diseases.* Franklin Watts, 1987
Edelson, Edward. *Genetics and Heredity.* Chelsea House, 1991
Facklam, Margery and Facklam, Howard. *Pharmacology: The Good Drugs.* Facts on File, 1992
—— *Spare Parts for People.* Harcourt Brace, 1987
Feinberg, Brian. *The Musculoskeletal System.* Chelsea House, 1994
Flanders, Stephen A. and Flanders, Carl N. *AIDS.* Facts on File, 1990
Hooper, Tony. *Genetics.* Raintree Steck-Vaughn, 1993
—— *Surgery.* Raintree Steck-Vaughn, 1993
Metos, Thomas H. *Communicable Diseases.* Franklin Watts, 1987
Murphy, Wendy and Murphy, Jack. *Nuclear Medicine.* Chelsea House, 1994
Nourse, Allen E. *Sexually Transmitted Diseases.* Franklin Watts, 1992
—— *The Virus Invaders.* Franklin Watts, 1992
Parker, Steve. *The Brain and Nervous System.* Franklin Watts, 1991
—— *The Heart and Blood.* Franklin Watts, 1991
Senior, Kathryn. *Medicine: Doctors, Demons and Drugs.* Franklin Watts, 1993
Silverstein, Alvin, et al. *Common Cold and Flu.* Enslow, 1994
Stewart, Gail B. *Alternative Healing: Opposing Viewpoints.* Greenhaven, 1990

INDEX

*Index numerals appearing in **Boldface** indicate caption references.*

© Evans Brothers Limited 1994